How to Make Wooden Baskets

by
John Nelson
and
William Guimond

Fox Chapel Publishing Co., Inc.
1970 Broad Street
East Petersburg, PA 17520

Publisher: Alan Giagnocavo
Project Editor: Ayleen Stellhorn
Desktop Specialist: Robert Altland, Altland Design

ISBN 1-56523-099-X

We wish to thank Michael Dumont for the instructional photographs, Colette Guimond for her beautiful lid design and instructions, Joyce Nelson for typing the book manuscript and Alan Giagnocavo and staff at Fox Chapel Publishing Company, Inc. Without their help this book could not have been published. For other basket patterns, call Scroller, Ltd. at 1-800-486-6053.

To order your copy of this book,
please send check or money order
for $9.95 plus $2.50 shipping to:
Fox Chapel Book Orders
1970 Broad Street
East Petersburg, PA 17520

Try your favorite book supplier first!

Table of Contents

Basic Instructions

The following pages have step-by-step photographs and instructions for you to make a simple country scroll saw basket. These instructions are written specifically for this basket design. All other baskets in this book are made using the exact same steps.

The basket patterns included in this book are only a beginning. Use your imagination to create hundreds of other designs of your own: add layers to increase the height of your basket, use thicker or thinner layers for different effects, enlarge or reduce the pattern for a particular need, use different kinds of wood to change the look of your basket. In doing this, you will create a basket that is truly *your* design. The combinations you can use are endless.

Finishing Your Basket

We recommend leaving the finished baskets with no finish at all on them, just their natural wood. If, however, you wish to stain or apply a satin finish coat of varnish to your basket, use any available commercial stain or varnish product that you would apply on any other woodworking project. Apply per instructions on the container. For ease, try to use a spray top coat; it will speed up your work.

Suggested Materials

As with all scroll saw projects, always use high quality, knot-free wood. Recommended woods for baskets are aspen, basswood or poplar. They are hardwoods and cut easily on the scroll saw. Most soft woods are not recommended because they have little "character." To add trim or color variations use mahogany, cherry, maple or red oak. For example, you may choose to use a maple wood for the base, top rim and handle, then use a mahogany wood for the levels of the basket.

Step 1: Enlarge/Reduce Pattern

• Decide what size basket you wish to make.

• Use a photocopier to enlarge or reduce the pattern to suit your needs or to fit the size of wood that you plan to use. Try to have the copy made in red. A red line is easier to follow than a black line.

• Be sure to make enough copies to complete all layers (especially if you do not stack-cut). We recommend you make an extra copy or two, just in case.

Note: If you'd like to make the same basket the authors are making in this how-to sequence, use the patterns on pages 13–16 for a large basket or those on pages 18–19.

Step 2: Attaching Pattern to Wood

• Add one quarter of an inch to the required size and cut the wood to the overall size.

• Sand the top of the block lightly before applying the pattern.

• Glue the copy of the pattern to the wood using either rubber cement or a spray adhesive. Be sure to apply the glue spray to the paper pattern, not the wood. Allow the glue or adhesive to get tacky before applying the pattern to the wood, so that it can be easily removed later.

Step 3: Setting the Saw Blade

• Before starting, check that the blade is at a precise 90-degree angle to the table top. This is very important.

• Use a #2 skip tooth or regular blade for most baskets. (You may choose another blade based on your own preferences.)

• If you make a very small basket, use a #0/2 blade.

Step 4: Cut Base

• Attach the base pattern to the wood.

• Carefully cut out the base. Use a #2 blade and try to split the line as you cut.

• Round the bottom edge of the base using a $1/8$ inch or $3/16$ inch round over bit in a router. (This step is optional.)

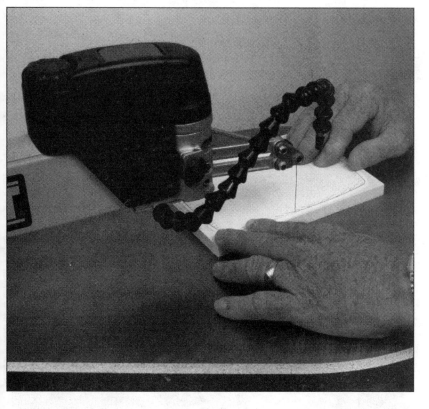

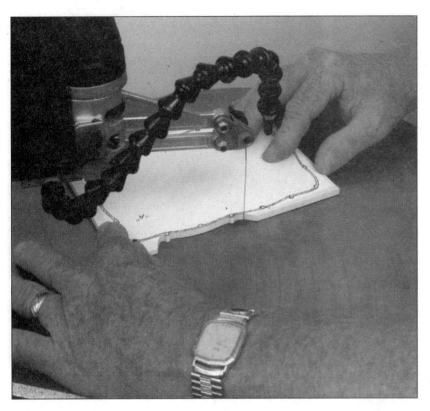

Step 5: Cut Level A

• Attach the Level A pattern to the wood.

• Carefully cut out this piece. Use a #2 blade and try to split the line as you cut.

• Cut the outside first and then drill a starter hole for the inside cut.

• Keep the center section intact to aid you in sanding the bottom surface. (See Step 9.)

• When removing the pattern from the wood, be sure to transfer the alignment dot to the wood surface. Use a pencil or pen and keep it small.

Step 5 (Optional): Stack-Cutting Level A

• Cut all pieces of wood required for Level A.

• Using a blank sheet of paper slightly larger than the wood, spray one side with adhesive. When the adhesive is tacky, adhere the blank sheet to the wood, then spray the top of the paper with more adhesive. When that adhesive is tacky, apply the second layer of wood. Repeat these steps for the remaining layers, until all required pieces are in a neat stack. (Try not to go over 1½ inches in height.)

• When complete, attach the Level A pattern to the top piece of wood.

• Carefully cut out the pieces. Use a #2 blade and try to split the line.

• When removing the pattern from the wood be sure to transfer the alignment dot to the wood surface. Use a pencil or pen and keep it small.

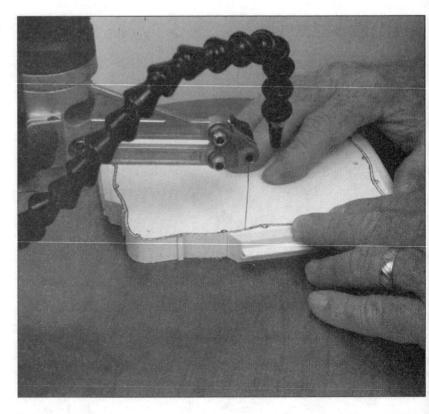

Step 6: Cut Level B (Single Level)

• Attach the level B pattern to the wood.
• Carefully cut out the piece. Use a #2 blade and try to split the line.
• Cut the outside first and drill a starter hole for the inside cut. Keep the center section intact to aid in sanding the bottom surface. (See Step 9.)
• When removing the pattern from the wood be sure to transfer the alignment dot to the wood surface. Use a pencil or pen and keep it small.

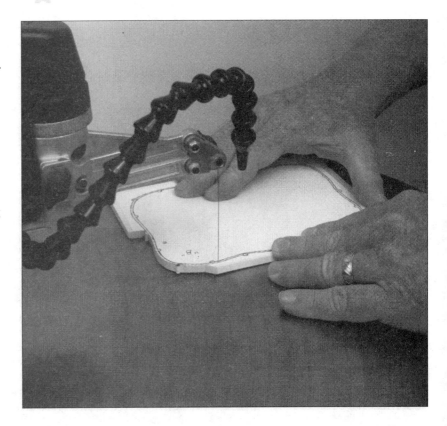

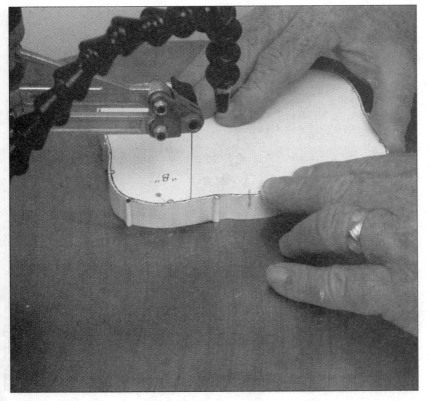

Step 6 (Optional): Stack-Cutting Level B

• Cut all pieces of wood required for Level B.
• Using a blank sheet of paper slightly larger than the wood, spray one side with adhesive. When the adhesive is tacky, adhere the blank paper to the wood, then spray the top of the paper with more adhesive. When that adhesive is tacky, apply the second layer of wood. Repeat these steps for the remaining layers, until all required pieces are in a neat stack. (Try not to go over $1^1/2$ inches in height.)
• When complete, attach the Level B pattern to the top piece of wood.
• Carefully cut out the pieces. Use a #2 blade and try to split the line.
• When removing the pattern from the wood be sure to transfer the alignment dot to the wood surface. Use a pencil or pen and keep it small.

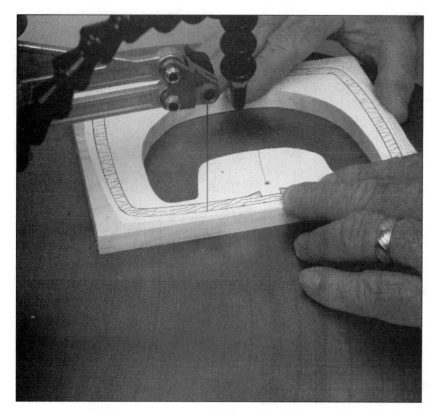

Step 7: Cut Top Rim

- Attach the pattern to the wood.
- Remove the handle portion from the center of the pattern.
- Carefully cut out the piece. Use a #2 or #5 blade and try to split the line.
- If the top rim has a notch for the handle, be sure the notch is the same *width* as the handle thickness. This is a very important part of this step.

Step 8: Cut Handle, Fit to Rim

- Using the handle portion that was removed from the rim pattern center section, carefully cut out the piece. Use a #2 blade for small interior cuts and an optional #5 blade for the handle portion. Try to split the pattern line as you make the cuts.

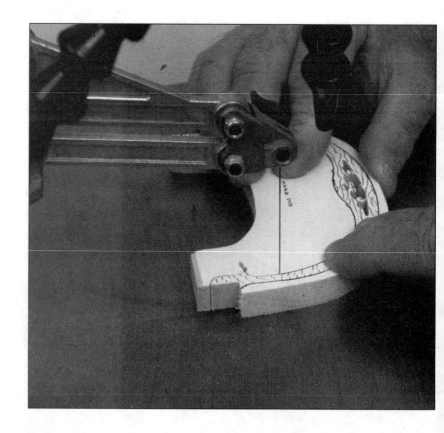

Step 9: Sand the Front/Back Surfaces

• Take a piece of #150 grit sandpaper and put it on a flat surface.

• Reinsert the center portion to support the layer while you are sanding.

• Lightly sand each piece of the basket to remove any burrs.

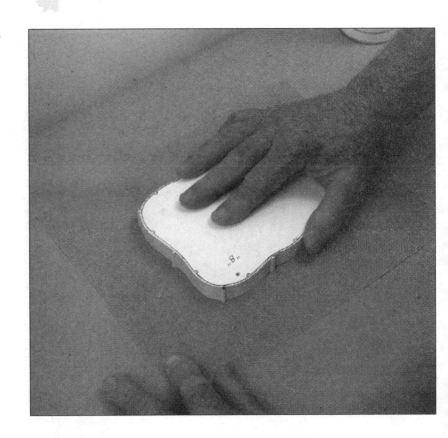

Step 10: Glue Level A to Base

• Remove the pattern and transfer the alignment dot. Note: If a problem occurs in removing the pattern, use a hairdryer and heat the surface. The pattern will then lift easily from the wood.

• Carefully put a small dab of white glue at each "stay," about 2 or 3 inches apart, keeping the alignment dot in an "up" position.

• Center the piece on the base.

• Wipe off any excess glue.

• Let the basket sit for 5–10 minutes under a weight to keep it flat.

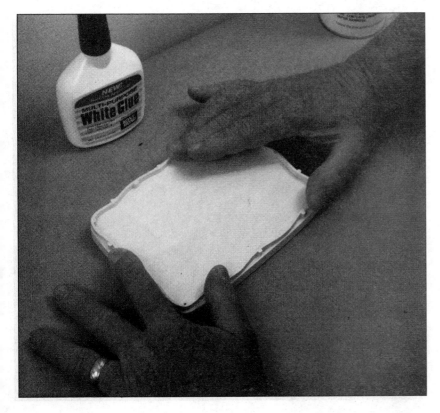

Step 11: Glue Level B to Level A

• Continue gluing the pieces together. Put a small dab of white glue every 2–3 inches apart at each stay on Level B.
• Add the next level, lining up the alignment dots.
• Wipe off any excess glue.
• Let the basket sit for 5–10 minutes under a weight.
• Repeat these steps, alternating the layers until all the layers are stacked.

Step 12: Add the Top Rim and Handle

• Glue the handle to the rim in the groove provided. Keep the handle at a 90-degree angle to the rim.
• Glue the top rim and handle assembly, centered, to the top level of the basket.
• Clamp or weight the pieces until the glue is dry. Remove any excess glue.
• Lightly sand the entire basket.
• Finish the basket to suit. (You can leave your basket unfinished, stain it or paint it.)

Step 13: Completed Basket

Basket Variations

Each basket can be enlarged or reduced. You can add or remove various levels, add handles, leave handles off or add lids to design your very own basket. You are limited only by your imagination.

Basket Patterns

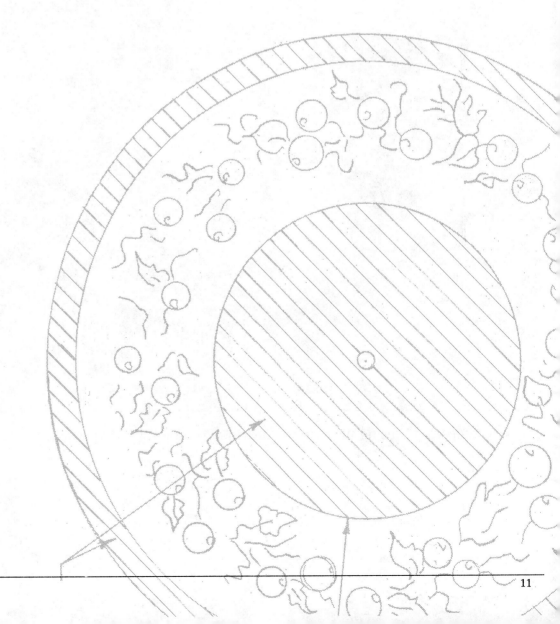

Large Market Basket

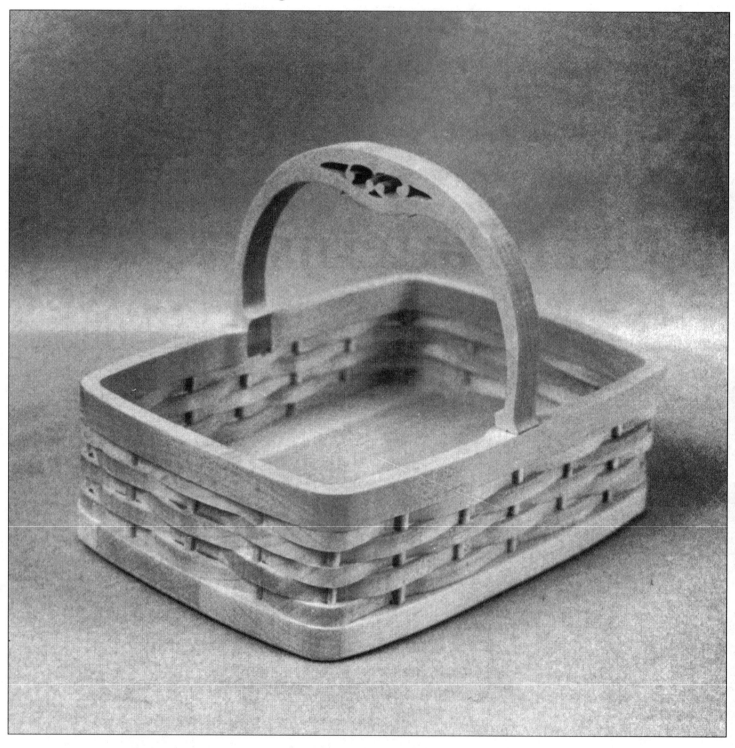

Follow Steps 1–13, using the patterns provided on the following pages.

Optional ³/₁₆"–¹/₄" radius bottom edge.

Base—¹/₂" thick. Cut one (required).

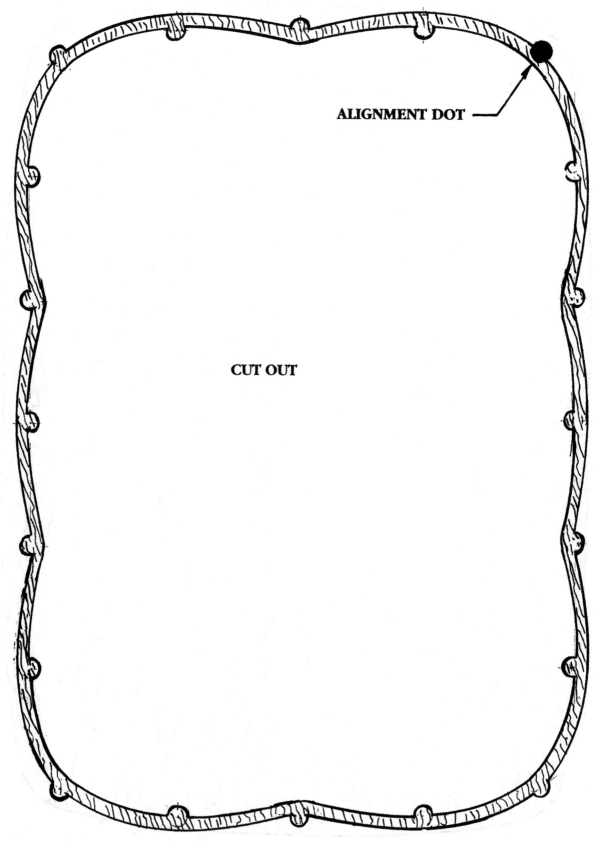

ALIGNMENT DOT

CUT OUT

Level A—1/4" thick. Cut three (suggested).

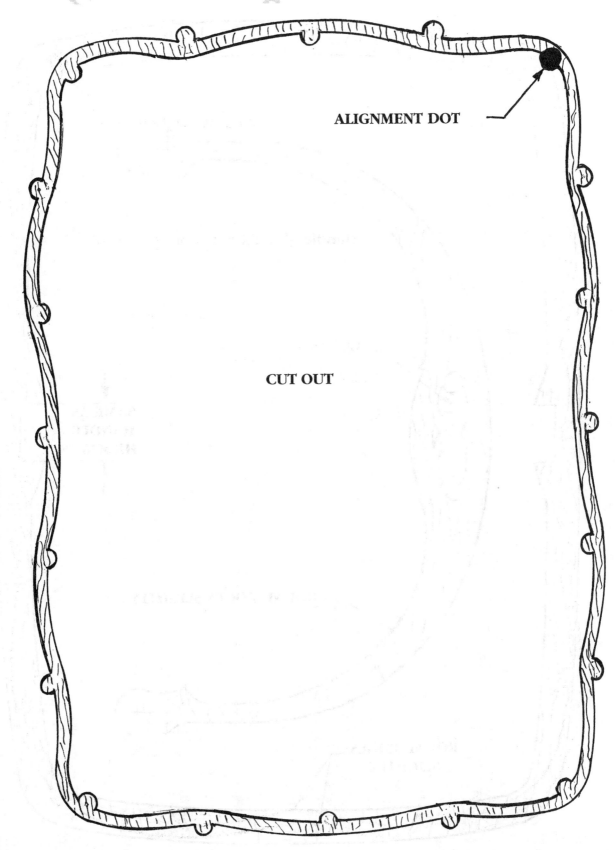

ALIGNMENT DOT

CUT OUT

Level B—1/4" thick. Cut two (suggested).

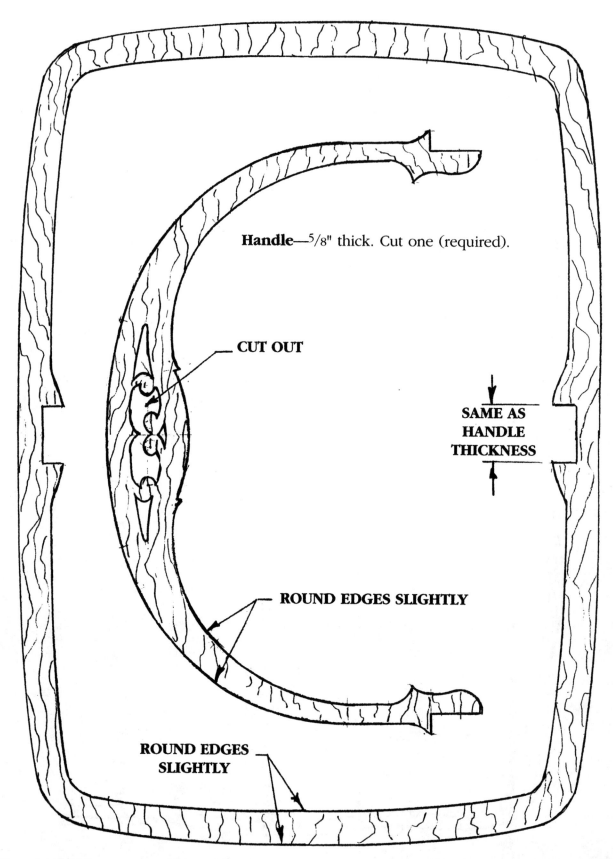

Handle—5/8" thick. Cut one (required).

CUT OUT

**SAME AS
HANDLE
THICKNESS**

ROUND EDGES SLIGHTLY

**ROUND EDGES
SLIGHTLY**

Top Rim—1/2" thick. Cut one (required).

Basic Patterns

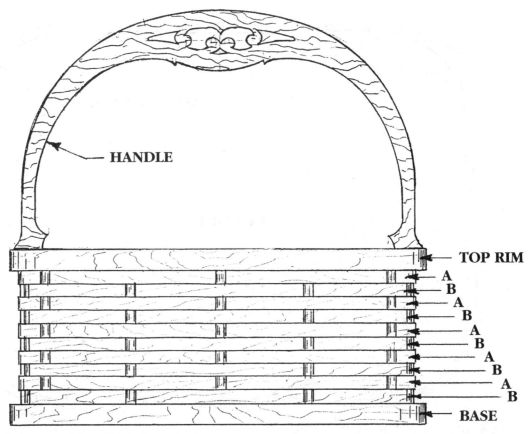

HANDLE

TOP RIM

A
B
A
B
A
B
A
B
A
B
A
B

BASE

Assembly View—Large and Small Market Baskets

Small Market Basket

Follow Steps 1–13, using the patterns on the following pages and the assembly view above.

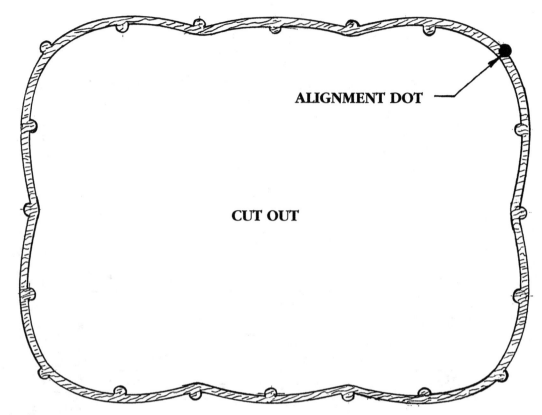

ALIGNMENT DOT

CUT OUT

Level A—1/4" thick. Cut three (suggested).

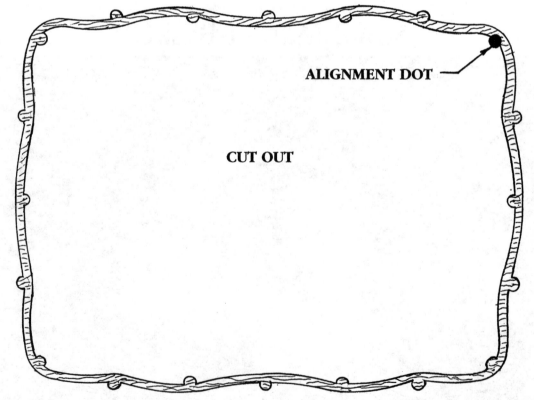

ALIGNMENT DOT

CUT OUT

Level B—1/4" thick. Cut three (suggested).

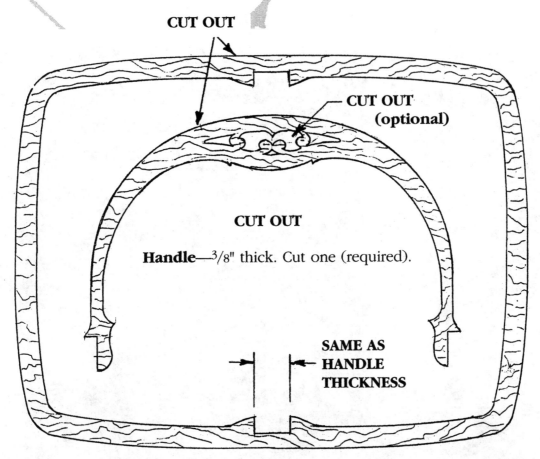

CUT OUT

CUT OUT (optional)

CUT OUT

Handle—³⁄₈" thick. Cut one (required).

SAME AS HANDLE THICKNESS

Top Rim—¹⁄₄" thick. Cut one (required).

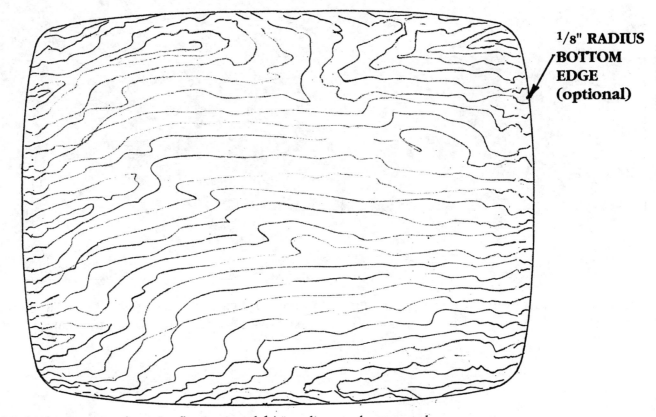

¹⁄₈" RADIUS BOTTOM EDGE (optional)

Base—¹⁄₄" thick. Cut one (required). Optional ¹⁄₈" radius on bottom edge.

Oval Basket

Follow steps 1 through 13, using the patterns on the following pages.
Stagger Levels A and B, one right-side-up, the next up-side-down, and so on, to create a woven effect.

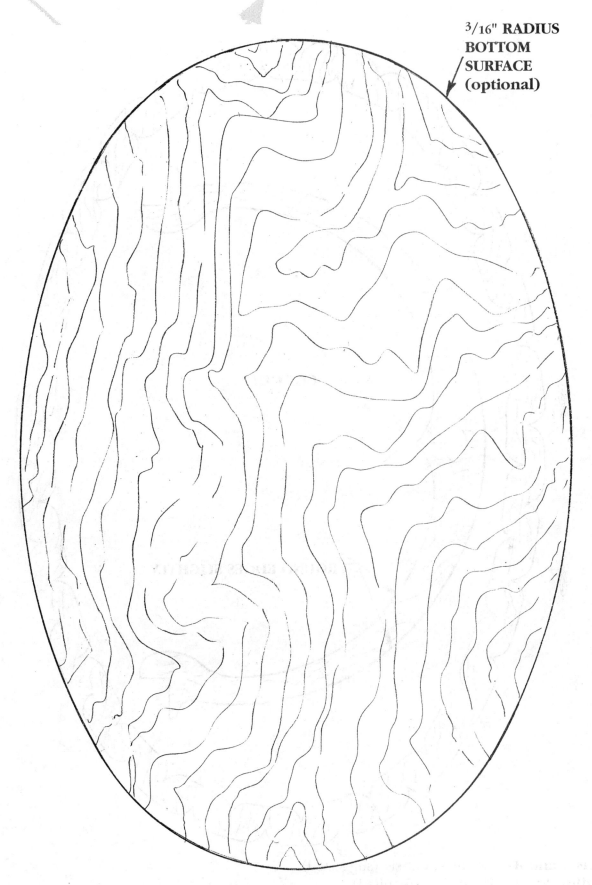

3/16" **RADIUS BOTTOM SURFACE** (optional)

Base—1/2" thick. Cut one (required). 3/16" radius on bottom surface only.

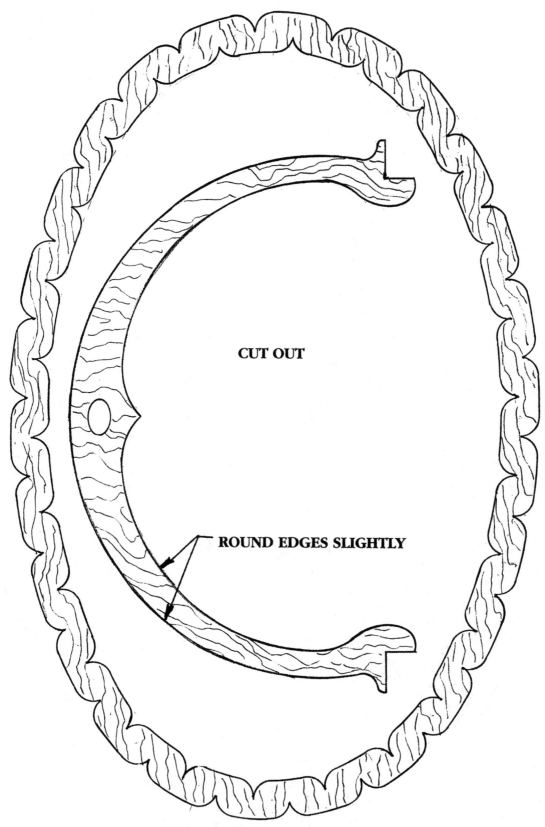

CUT OUT

ROUND EDGES SLIGHTLY

Levels A and B—1/2" thick. Cut six (suggested).
Handle—9/16" thick. Cut one (required).

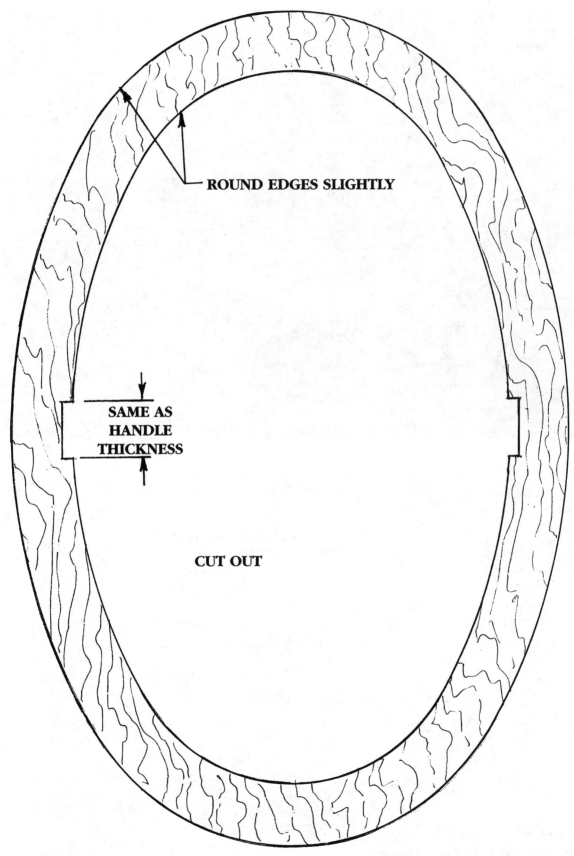

ROUND EDGES SLIGHTLY

SAME AS
HANDLE
THICKNESS

CUT OUT

Top Rim—1/2" thick. Cut one (required).

Small Oval Basket

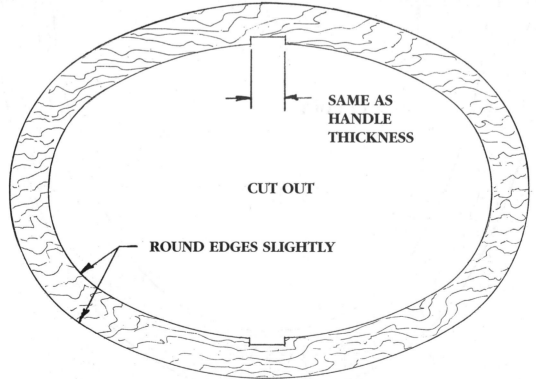

SAME AS HANDLE THICKNESS

CUT OUT

ROUND EDGES SLIGHTLY

Top Rim—¹/4" thick. Cut one (required).

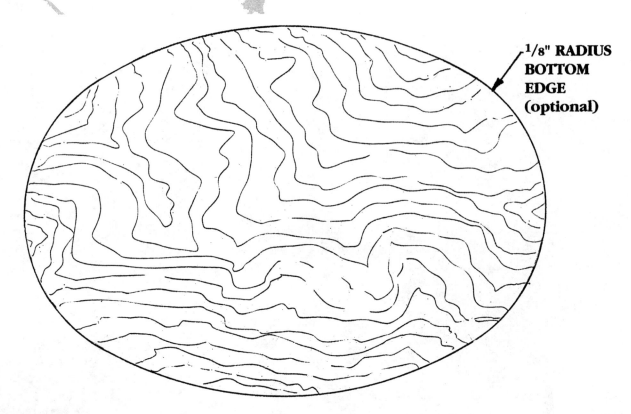

1/8" RADIUS BOTTOM EDGE (optional)

Base—1/4" thick. Cut one (required).

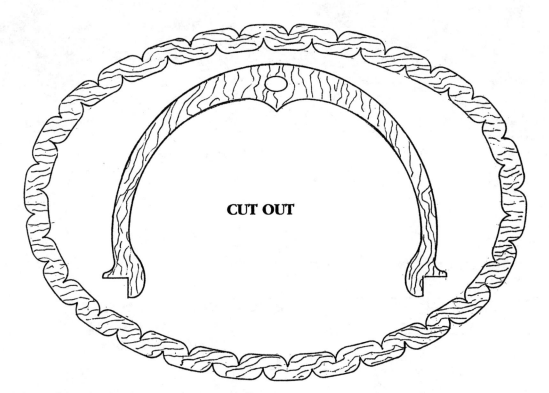

CUT OUT

Levels A and B—1/4" thick. Cut six (suggested).

Large Round Basket and Small Round Basket

Follow steps 1 through 13, using the patterns on the following pages.
Stagger each level to create a "brick" pattern.

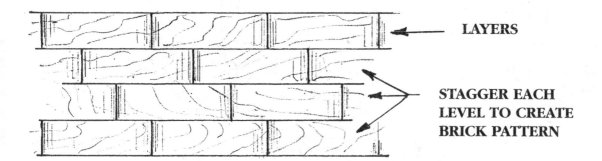

LAYERS

**STAGGER EACH
LEVEL TO CREATE
BRICK PATTERN**

Large Round Basket

ROUND BOTTOM EDGE SLIGHTLY

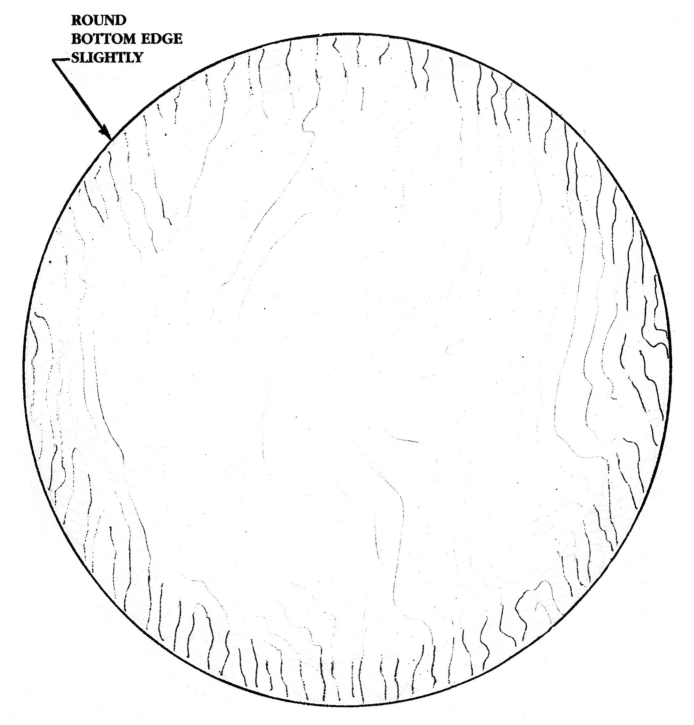

Base—1/4" thick. Cut one (required).

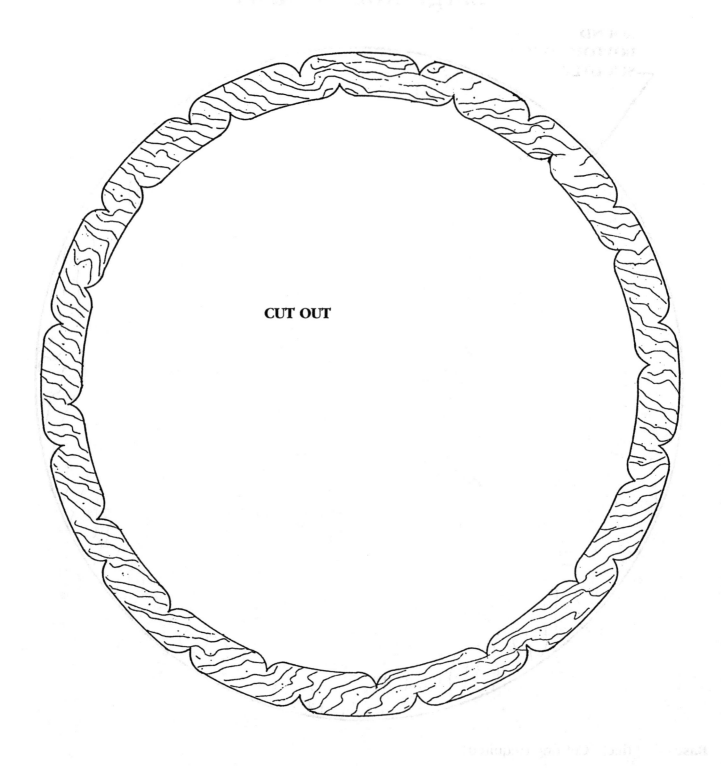

CUT OUT

Levels A and B—$1/2$" thick. Cut six (suggested).
Note: Stack levels as shown in the Illustration on page 26 to create a brick pattern.

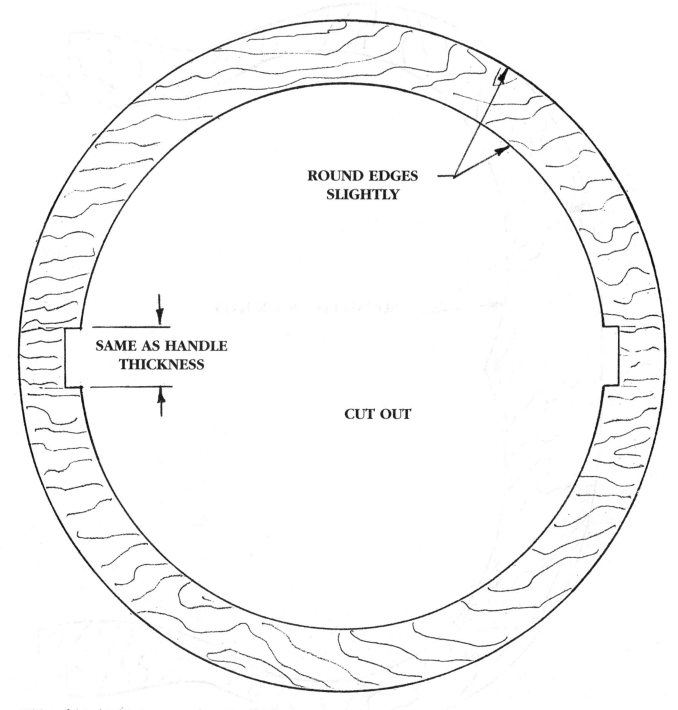

ROUND EDGES SLIGHTLY

SAME AS HANDLE THICKNESS

CUT OUT

Top Rim—1/4" thick. Cut one (required).

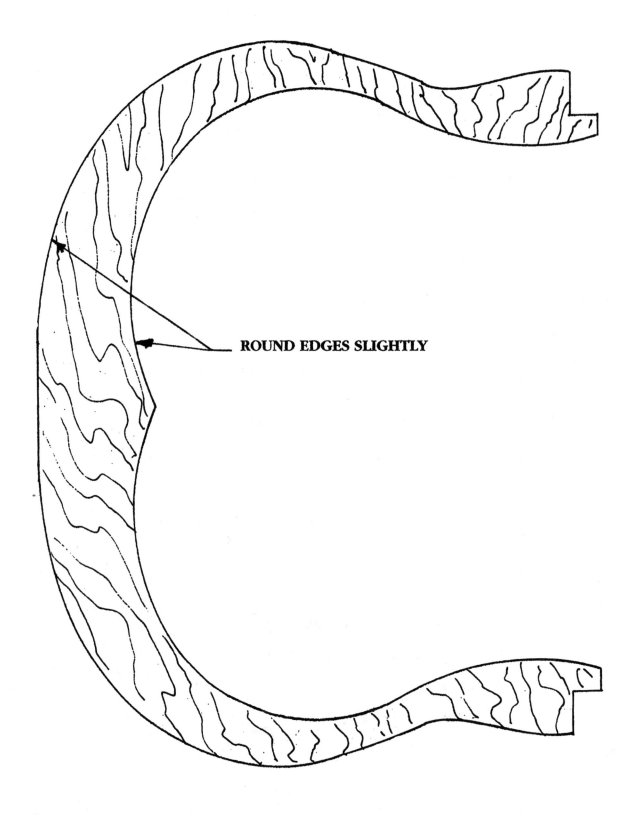

ROUND EDGES SLIGHTLY

Handle—5/8" thick. Cut one (required).

Small Round Basket

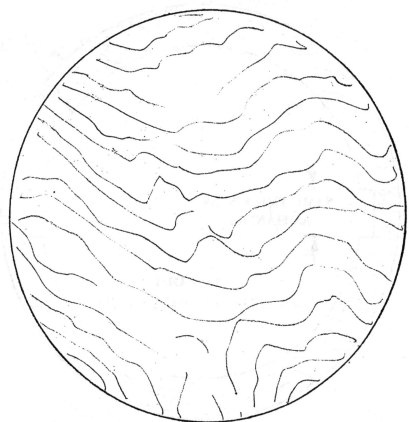

Base—1/4" thick. Cut one (required).

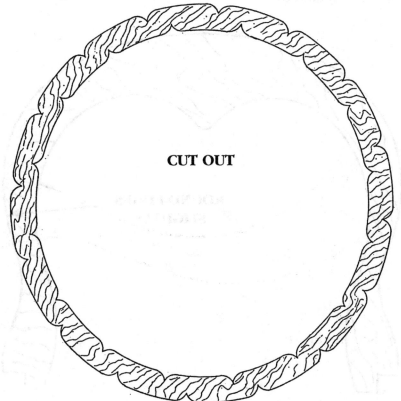

CUT OUT

Levels A and B—1/4" thick. Cut eight (suggested).
Note: Stack per Illustration on page 26 to create a brick pattern

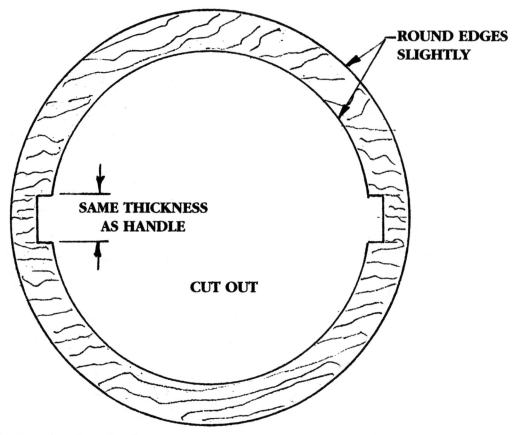

Top Rim—1/4" thick. Cut one (required).

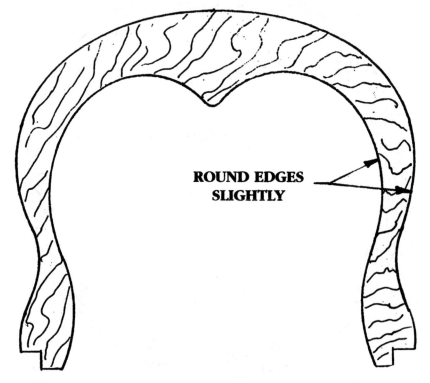

Handle—1/2" thick. Cut one (required).

Candy Dish

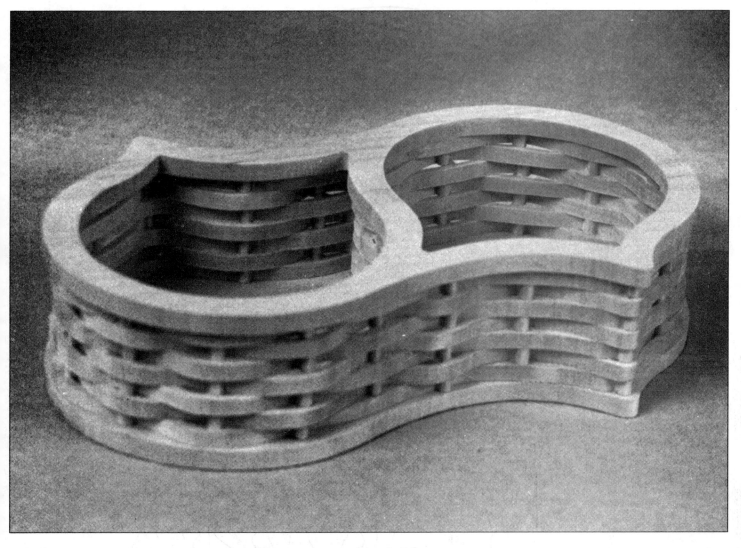

Follow steps 1 through 13, using the patterns on the following pages.
Glue up the levels as shown below.

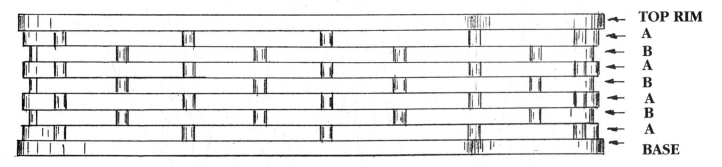

TOP RIM
A
B
A
B
A
B
A
BASE

Side View—Assembly

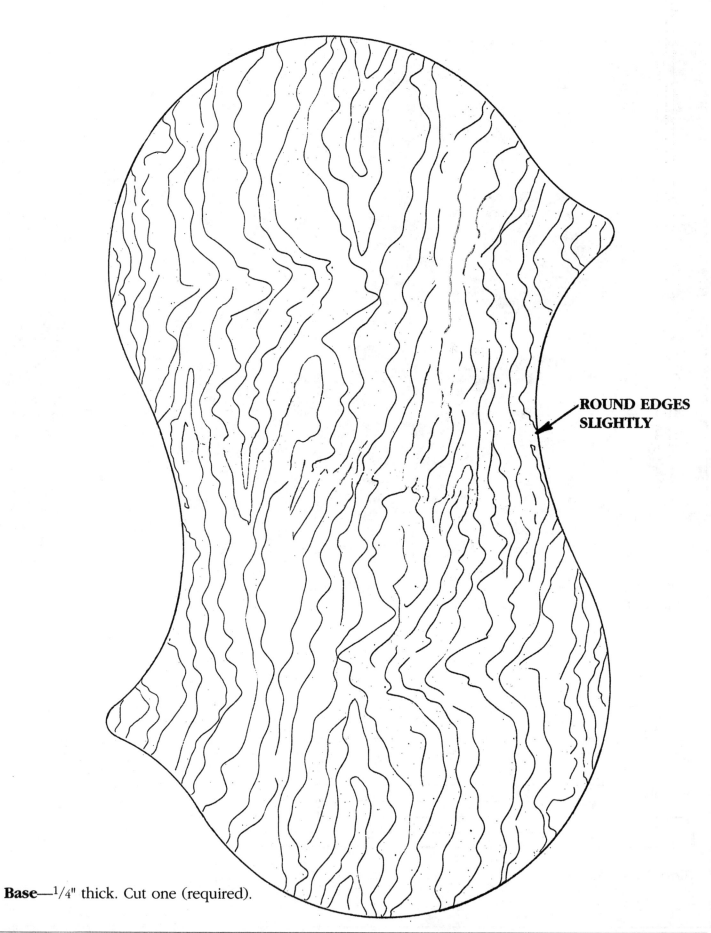

**ROUND EDGES
SLIGHTLY**

Base—1/4" thick. Cut one (required).

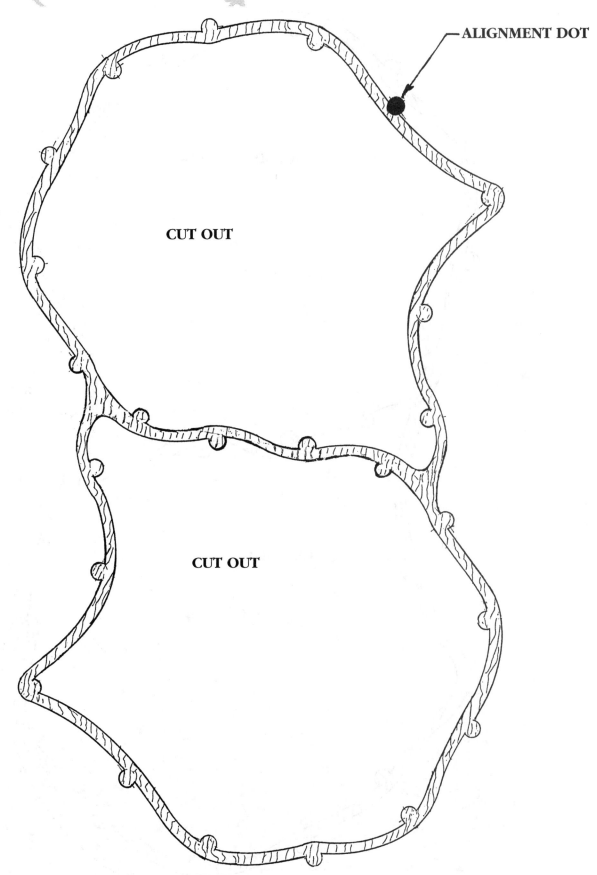

ALIGNMENT DOT

CUT OUT

CUT OUT

Level A—1/4" thick. Cut four (suggested).

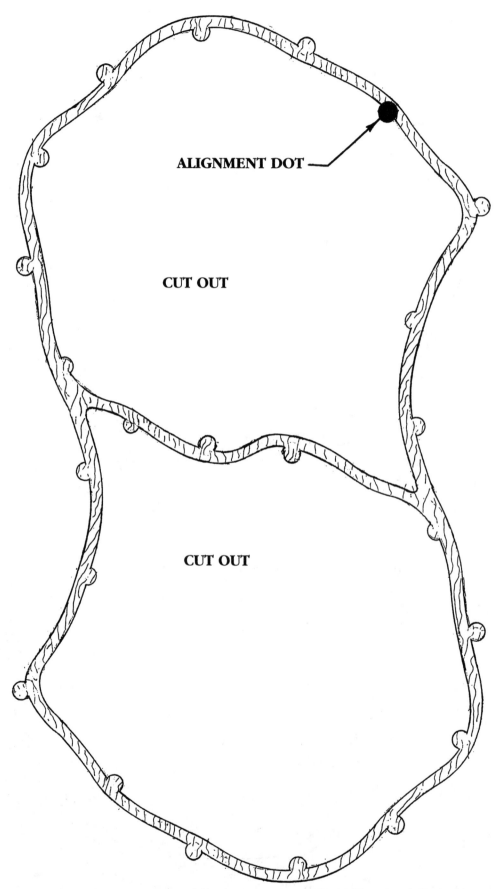

ALIGNMENT DOT ———

CUT OUT

CUT OUT

Level B—1/4" thick. Cut three (suggested).

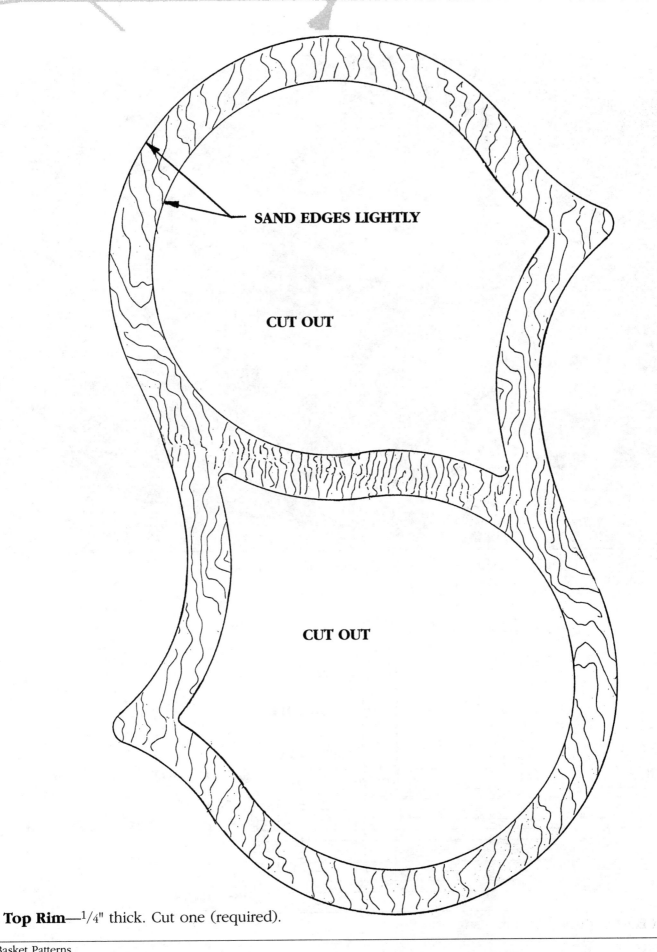

SAND EDGES LIGHTLY

CUT OUT

CUT OUT

Top Rim—1/4" thick. Cut one (required).

Square Basket

Follow steps 1 through 13, using the patterns on the following pages.
Use assembly view shown below as a guide.

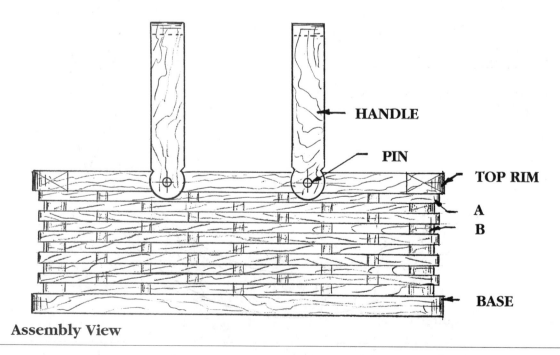

HANDLE

PIN

TOP RIM

A

B

BASE

Assembly View

Base—1/2" thick. Cut one (required). Round edges slightly.

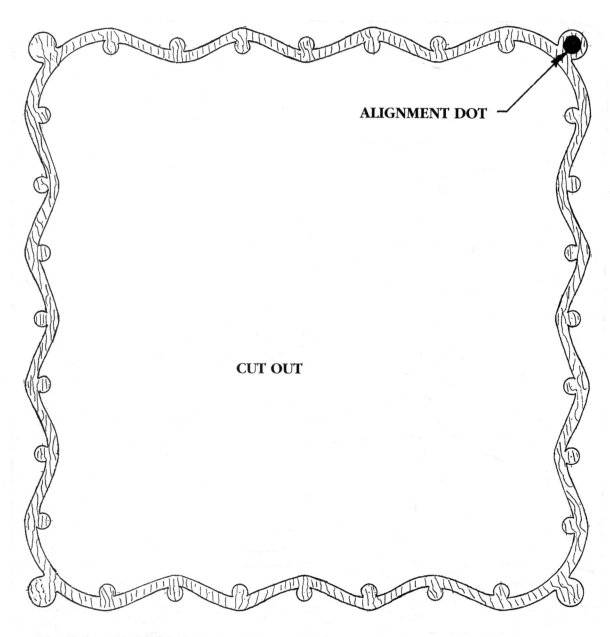

ALIGNMENT DOT

CUT OUT

Level A—1/4" thick. Cut four (suggested).

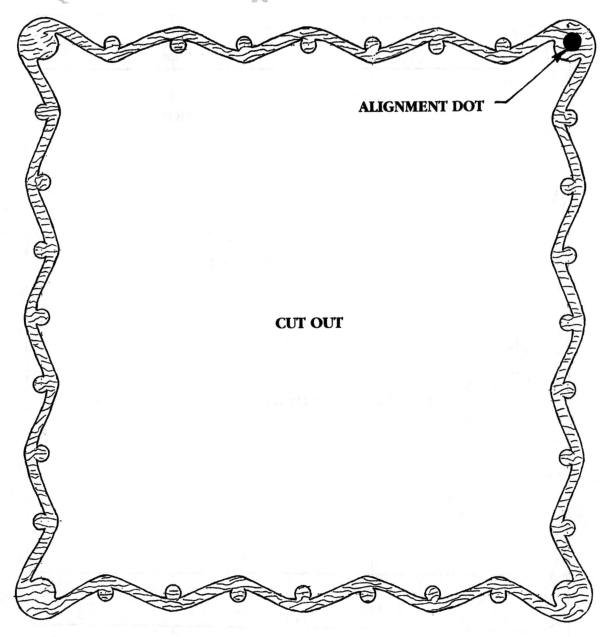

ALIGNMENT DOT

CUT OUT

Level B—1/4" thick. Cut three (suggested).

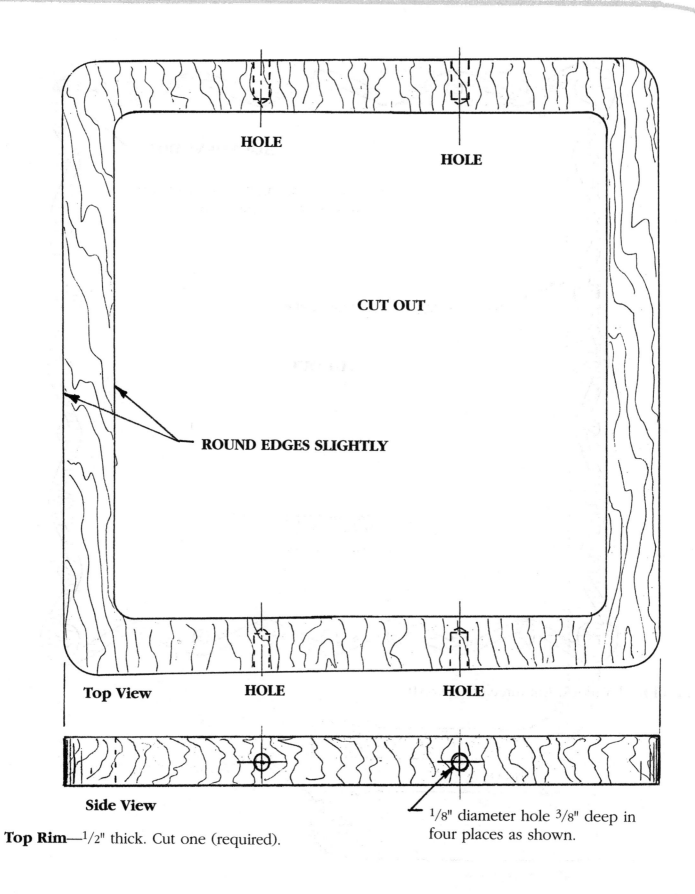

HOLE

HOLE

CUT OUT

ROUND EDGES SLIGHTLY

Top View

HOLE

HOLE

Side View

$^1/8"$ diameter hole $^3/8"$ deep in four places as shown.

Top Rim—$^1/2"$ thick. Cut one (required).

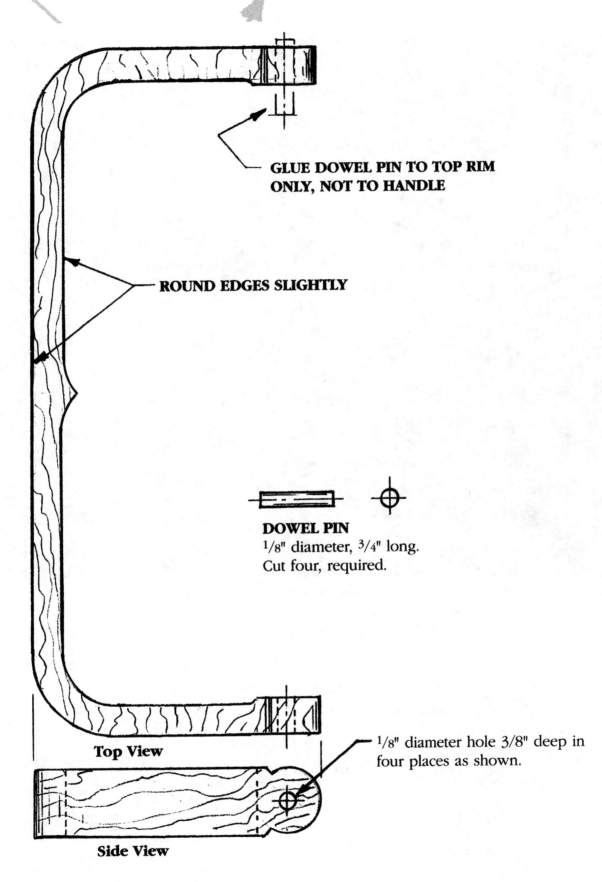

GLUE DOWEL PIN TO TOP RIM ONLY, NOT TO HANDLE

ROUND EDGES SLIGHTLY

DOWEL PIN
1/8" diameter, 3/4" long.
Cut four, required.

Top View

1/8" diameter hole 3/8" deep in four places as shown.

Side View

Handle—5/8" thick. Cut two (required).

Napkin Holder

Follow steps 1 through 13, using the patterns on the following pages.
Use the illustration below showing the side view of the assembly as a guide.
Note: For larger napkins increase the overall sizes of all of the patterns, 115% to 130%.

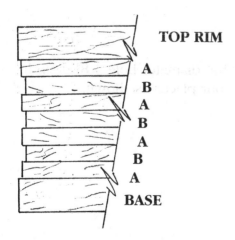

TOP RIM
A
B
A
B
A
B
A
B
A
BASE

Base—1/2" thick. Cut one (required). Round edges slightly.

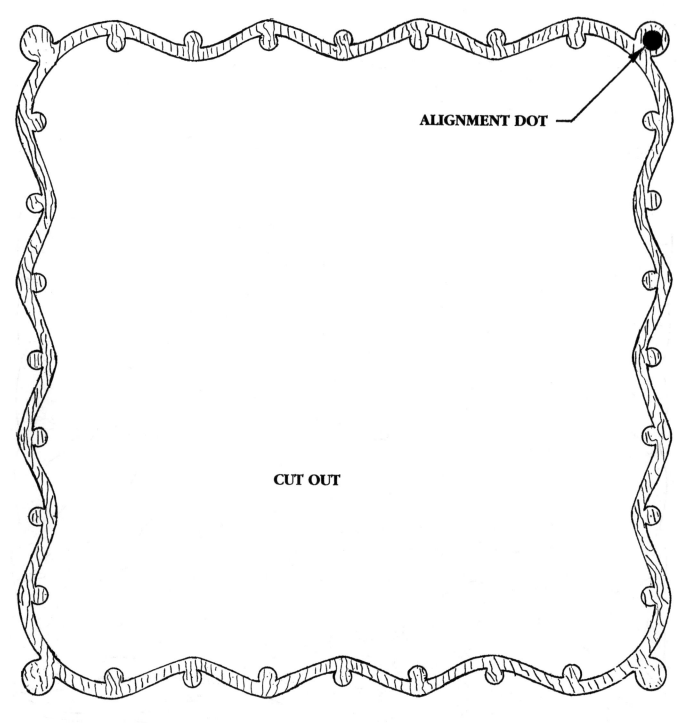

ALIGNMENT DOT —

CUT OUT

Level A—¹/4" thick. Cut four to six (suggested).

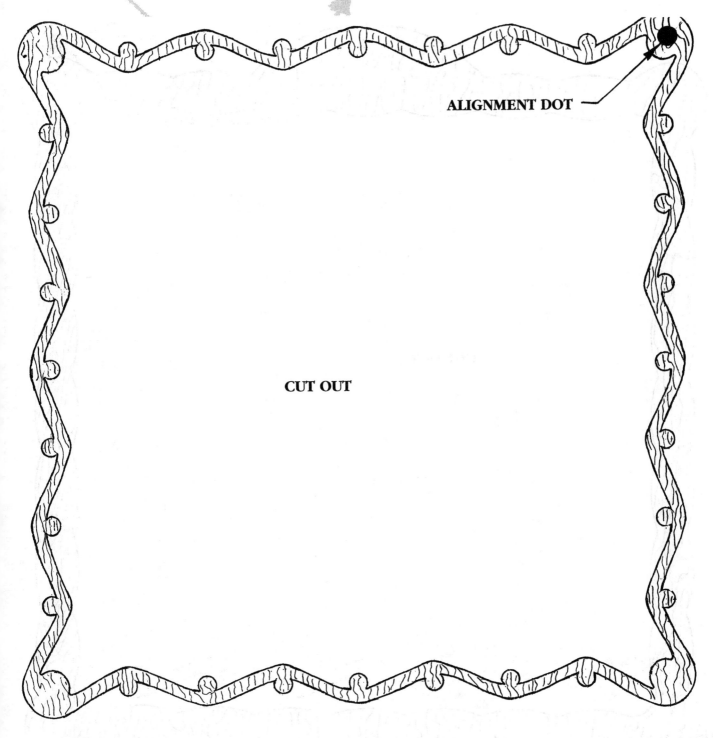

ALIGNMENT DOT

CUT OUT

Level B—$1/4$" thick. Cut three to five (suggested).

CUT OUT

Top Rim—$1/2$" thick. Cut one (required).

Tissue Box

Follow steps 1 through 13, using the patterns on the following pages.

Note: This design is based on a tissue box $4^1/8$" x $4^1/2$" x $5^1/2$" in size. Cut the top opening to match the opening in your tissue box.

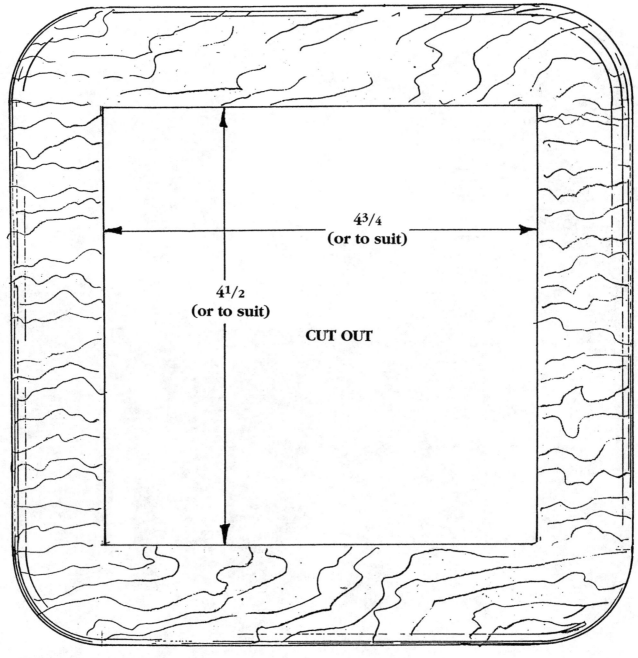

$4^3/4$
(or to suit)

$4^1/2$
(or to suit)

CUT OUT

Base—$1/4$" thick. Cut one (required).

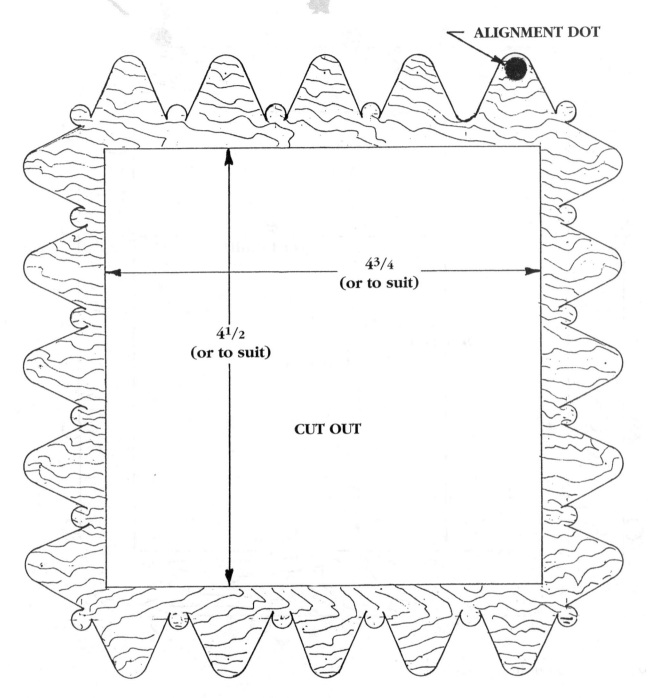

← ALIGNMENT DOT

$4^{3}/_{4}$
(or to suit)

$4^{1}/_{2}$
(or to suit)

CUT OUT

Level A—$^{1}/_{2}$" thick. Cut five (suggested)

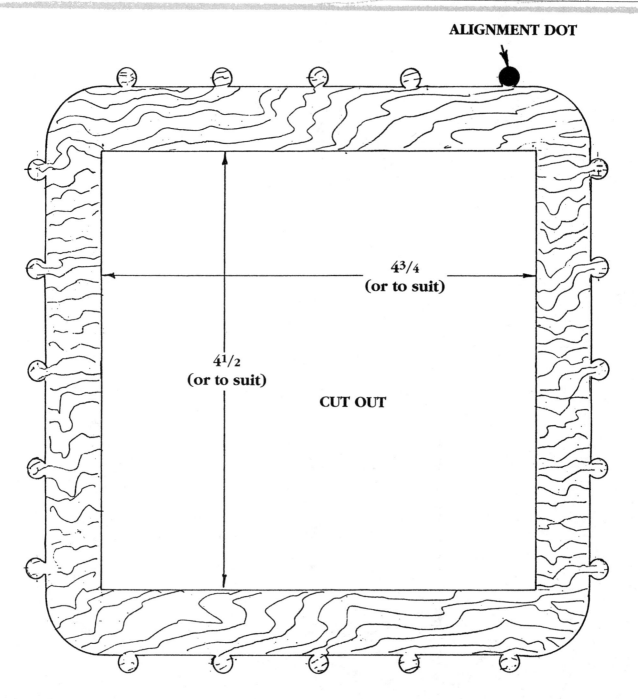

ALIGNMENT DOT

4³/₄
(or to suit)

4¹/₂
(or to suit)

CUT OUT

Level B—¹/₂" thick. Cut five (suggested).

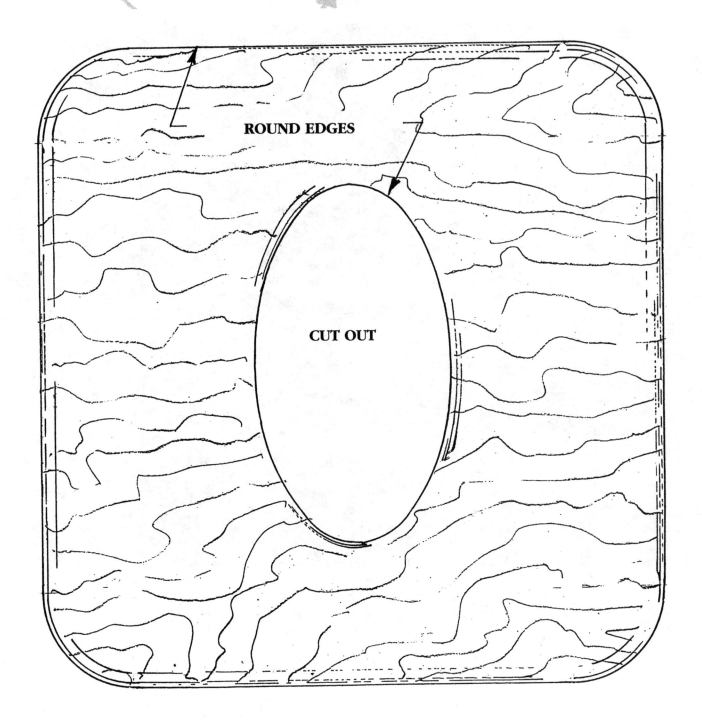

ROUND EDGES

CUT OUT

Top—1/4" thick. Cut one (required). Note: Cut hole in top to match opening in tissue box.

Round Basket with Lid

Follow steps 1 through 13, using the patterns on the following pages.

The lid can be left natural or tole painted. Instructions for painting the banded lid can be found on page 60.

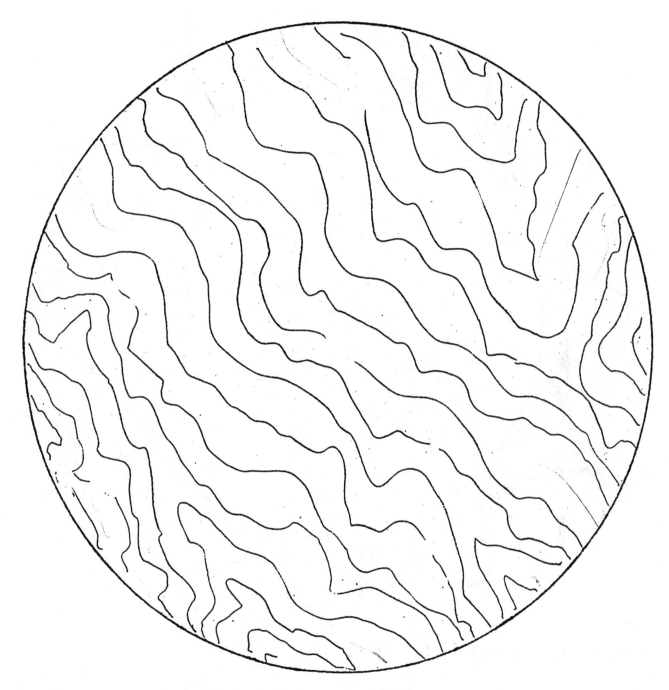

Base—1/4" thick. Cut one (required). Round bottom edge slightly

— ALIGNMENT DOT

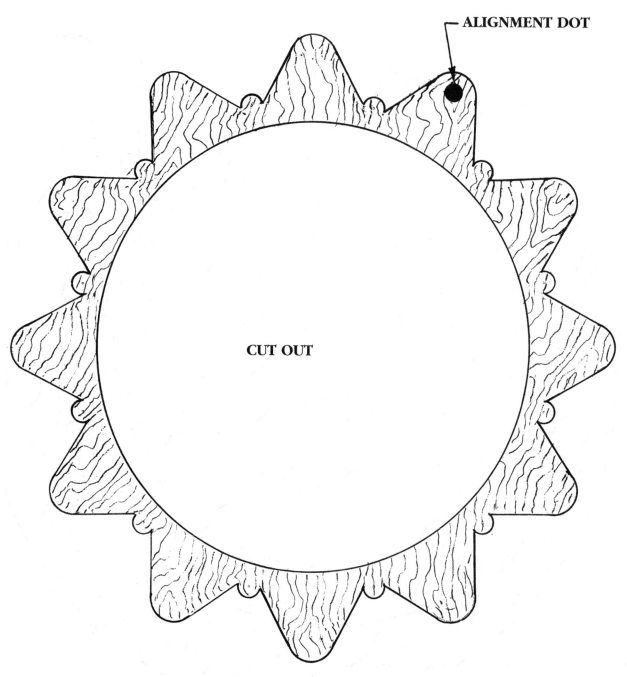

CUT OUT

Level A—1/2" thick. Cut three (suggested).

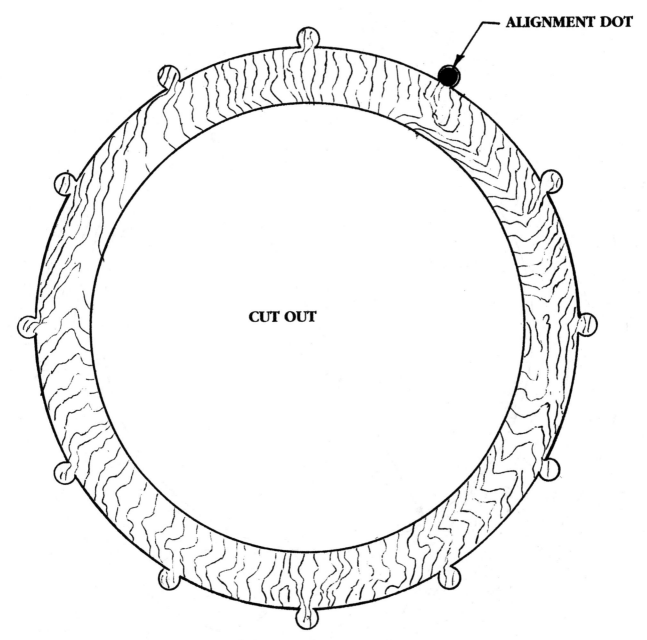

ALIGNMENT DOT

CUT OUT

Level B—1/2" thick. Cut two (suggested).

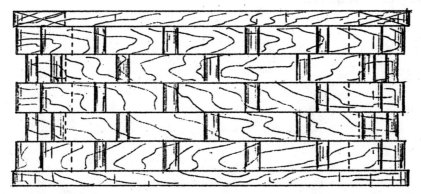

Assembly View without the lid.

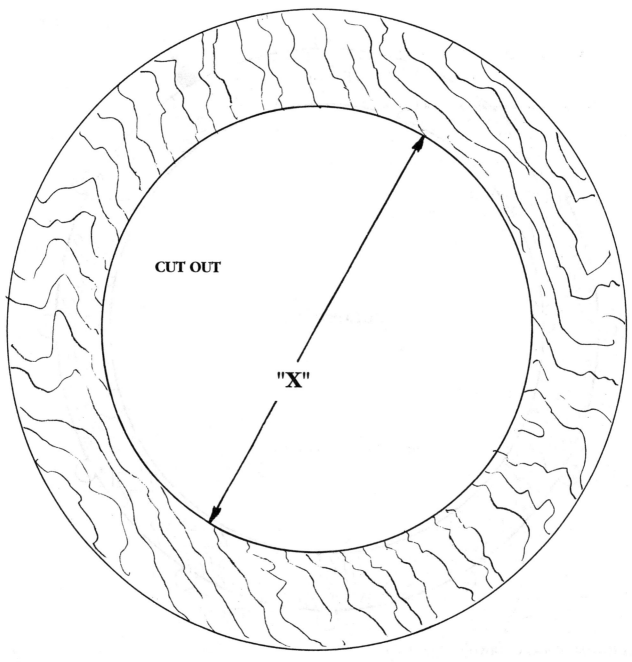

CUT OUT

"X"

Top Rim—1/4" thick. Cut one (required).

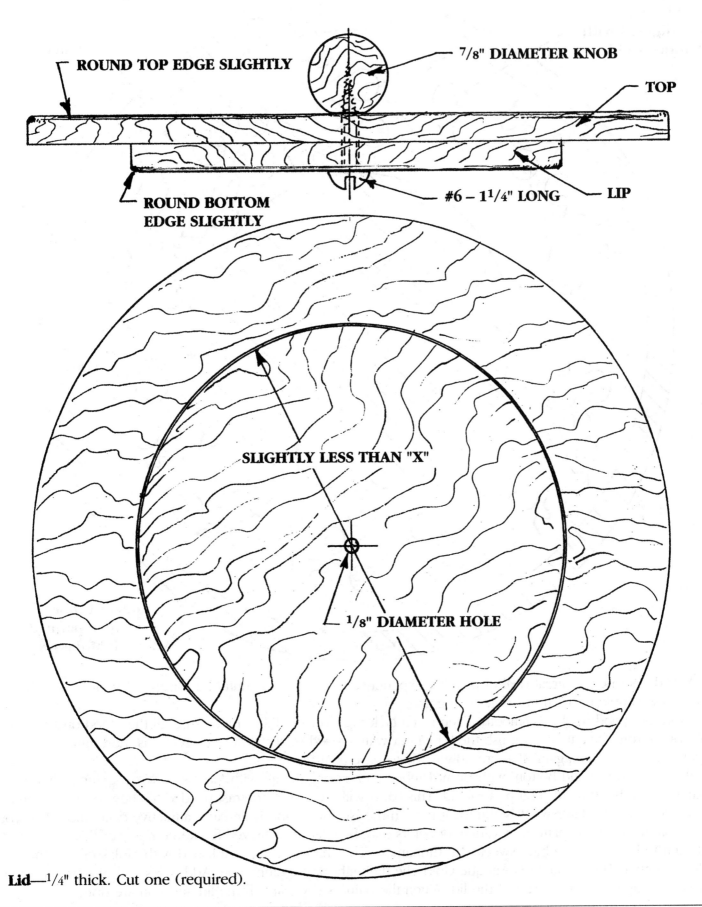

ROUND TOP EDGE SLIGHTLY

7/8" DIAMETER KNOB

TOP

ROUND BOTTOM EDGE SLIGHTLY

#6 – 1¹/4" LONG

LIP

SLIGHTLY LESS THAN "X"

1/8" DIAMETER HOLE

Lid—¹/4" thick. Cut one (required).

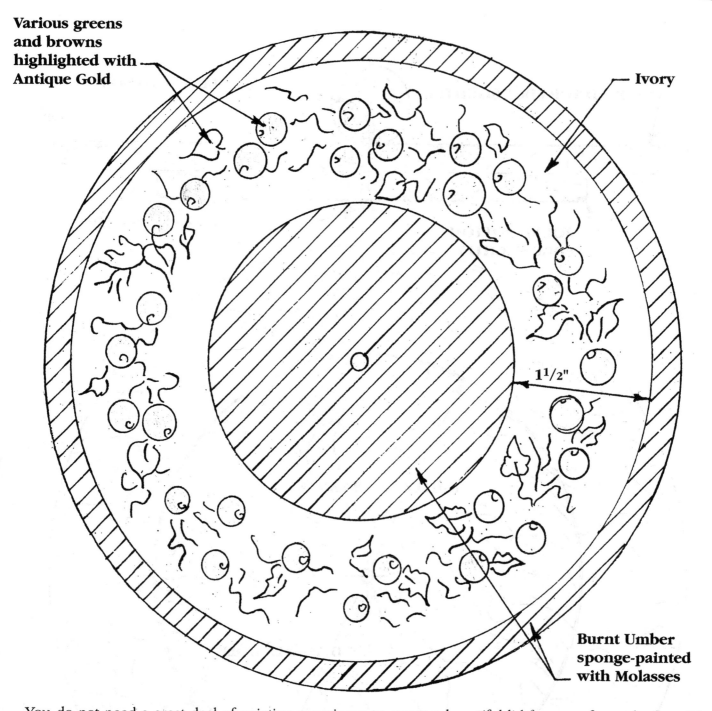

Various greens and browns highlighted with Antique Gold

Ivory

$1^{1}/_{2}$"

Burnt Umber sponge-painted with Molasses

You do not need a great deal of painting experience to create a beautiful lid for any of your baskets. Here are a few simple instructions to get you going.

Sand the wood until it is smooth. Then run a tack rag over the lid to make sure all the wood dust has been removed from the surface. Varnish the lid with a water-based sealer. When the sealer is thoroughly dry, sand and tack the surface again. You are now ready to base coat the lid.

Paint the lid top and bottom with Burnt Umber, then sponge paint with Molasses. When completely dry, paint a $1^{1}/_{2}$" Ivory band on top of the lid. This band will create the contrast needed to show off the bittersweet

Then have fun! Bittersweet is abundant here in the Northeast and is an easy, attractive decoration. Use your imagination with this pattern. A variety of colors may be used to achieve life-like berries. For this lid, I have chosen to base coat the bittersweet with Cinnamon. The shading is accomplished with Molasses and then Burnt Umber. The highlight is Antique Gold; the highlight dot is Cinnamon. Add twigs with the browns you have already used for the rest of the lid. When the paint is dry, varnish the lid and you are done.